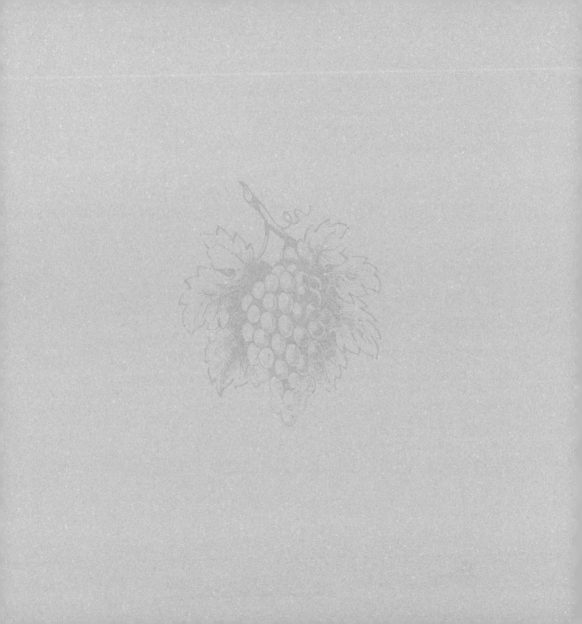

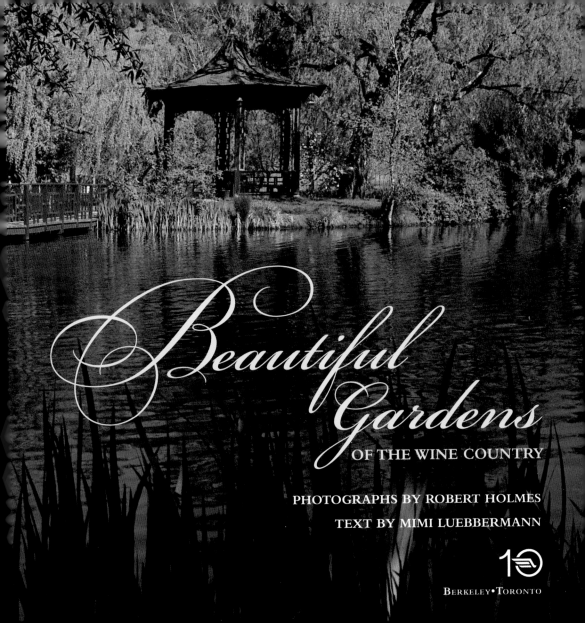

Beautiful
Gardens
OF THE WINE COUNTRY

PHOTOGRAPHS BY ROBERT HOLMES

TEXT BY MIMI LUEBBERMANN

BERKELEY•TORONTO

A Kirsty Melville book

Ten Speed Press
Box 7123
Berkeley, California 94707
www.tenspeed.com

Distributed in Australia by Simon & Schuster Australia, in Canada by Ten Speed Press Canada,
in New Zealand by Southern Publishers Group, in South Africa by Real Books, in Southeast Asia
by Berkeley Books, and in the United Kingdom and Europe by Airlift Book Company.

Concept and Design: Jennifer Barry Design, Fairfax, California
Photography: Robert Holmes, Sausalito, California
Text: Mimi Luebbermann
Layout Production: Kristen Wurz

The writer would like to extend warm thanks and appreciation to Jack Chandler,
of Jack Chandler & Associates, who has inspired and designed beautiful gardens of
the Wine Country for almost forty years.

Library of Congress Cataloging-in-Publication Data

Barry, Jennifer.
Beautiful gardens of wine country / by Jennifer Barry ;
photographs by Robert Holmes ; text by Mimi Luebbermann.
p. cm.
"A Kirsty Melville Book."
isbn 1-58008-638-1
1. Gardens—California, Northern. 2. Wineries—California, Northern.
I. Holmes, Robert, 1943– II. Luebbermann, Mimi. III. Title.
SB466.U65C22 2004
712'.09794'1—DC22
2004017626

Printed in China
10 9 8 7 6 5 4 3 2 1 — 08 07 06 05 04

Contents

*S*ome might question, which came first, the gardens or the vineyards? Only lately have wineries stumbled into gardening, realizing the value of the garden to enhance a visitor's pleasure. Like the great French chateaus and the Italian villas, gardens in the Wine Country have become part of the total experience of wine, whether as a stroll along a garden path, a kitchen garden for the winery chef, or an educational tool to teach affinities between varieties of wine and herbs, fruits and vegetables.

The proliferation of wineries built in the last thirty years has produced what some might call a helter-skelter accumulation of architectural styles and gardens. While a hidebound traditionalist might be shocked at the clash of garden cultures, a true garden voyager exults in this mélange of gardens. Visits to gardens featuring roses can be followed by those built around water features, or ones with terraces exhibiting sculptures by internationally known artists. Many wineries offer garden tours as well as winery tours.

In a small geographical space, the Northern California Wine Country encompasses a myriad of microclimates, from mild winters and foggy summers to areas with cold pockets and steaming-hot summer days. All the Wine Country gardens must face up to the long summer drought, with the first rains starting at the end of October, and the spring rains stopping in April. The intervening thirsty-long, six months will destroy a garden without regular irrigation and the inventive use of drought-tolerant plants or native California species.

The variety of microclimates allows different types of grapes to thrive, so that, unlike regions in Europe, where only one variety of grape grows in a large area, the Wine Country produces many different superb wines. Of course, the climate that so blesses the grapes equally benefits the gardens. The variety of plants arrayed in the gardens offers stunning proof of this diversity. So enjoy the beautiful gardens of the Wine Country. Laid out before you in a small geographical area are gardens you would otherwise have to travel the world to explore.

Garden Themes

previous pages and above: The gardens of Matanzas Creek Winery
and Estate Gardens, Santa Rosa, Sonoma Valley, feature a stunning garden
design using lavender, grasses, and native plants.

Ever since the Garden of Eden, humankind has been trying to order the natural landscape. Over time, gardens have developed from the practical necessity of growing food for the table to the spectacular rearrangement of land and trees, punctuated by water or sculpture for pure sensual and visual pleasure.

The emigrants to the Wine Country brought their own cultural sensibilities to the region. Yet climate and soil have their requirements, so as you stroll, study the themes with these two elements in mind.

A garden's bones—paths, water features, walls, and planting beds—lead the traveler through space, nurturing the senses with color, texture, and fragrance. As much as wine feeds the body, the garden feeds the soul.

LEFT: THE FORMAL GARDENS OF CHATEAU SOUVERAIN WINERY, GEYSERVILLE, ALEXANDER VALLEY,
FEATURE INTENSELY COLORFUL PLANTINGS OF ANNUALS.

ABOVE: THE GARDENS OF DOMAINE CARNEROS, NAPA, CARNEROS, REFLECT EUROPEAN FORMALITY
IN ITS GEOMETRIC PERFECTION.

FOLLOWING PAGES: THE LARGE FORMAL GARDENS OF NEWTON VINEYARD, ST. HELENA,
NAPA VALLEY, MIGHT BE TRANSPORTED FROM A FRENCH CHATEAU GARDEN WITH BANKS OF FLOWERS
EDGED BY SQUARED EVERGREENS OR SCULPTED SHRUBS.

ABOVE: PLANT-FILLED URNS FLANK A WALKWAY AT V. SATTUI WINERY, ST. HELENA, NAPA VALLEY.

LEFT AND FOLLOWING PAGES: TIGHTLY TRIMMED BOXWOOD HEDGES FORM ENCLOSING WALLS FOR PARTERRES,

CREATING THE GEOMETRIC SHAPES FIRST USED IN EUROPEAN GARDENS. CORKSCREW TRIMMED

EVERGREENS AND CYPRESS COMPLETE THE CLASSIC LOOK AT NEWTON VINEYARD, ST. HELENA, NAPA VALLEY.

PREVIOUS PAGES: CLOS PEGASE, CALISTOGA, NAPA
VALLEY. FORMAL EVERGREEN COLUMNS ENCLOSE A LAWN
AREA AND FRAME A VIEW OF THE BUILDING
AND THE CENTRALLY LOCATED TREE.
LEFT: ASIAN-INSPIRED GARDEN ORNAMENTATION AT
NEWTON VINEYARD, ST. HELENA, NAPA VALLEY.
ABOVE: A RED BRIDGE LEADS TO THE PAGODA-STYLE
GARDEN FOLLY ON AN ISLAND IN JADE LAKE AT
CHATEAU MONTELENA, CALISTOGA, NAPA VALLEY.

ABOVE AND RIGHT: THE JAPANESE-STYLED GARDENS OF OSMOSIS—THE ENZYME BATH SPA,
FREESTONE, SONOMA COUNTY, ARE MEANT TO EVOKE A CONTEMPLATIVE MOOD SUITABLE FOR REBUILDING
THE REPOSE OF BOTH MIND AND BODY. THE GARDENS ARE OPEN ONLY TO CLIENTS OF THE SPA.

PREVIOUS PAGES, ABOVE, AND RIGHT: FERRARI–CARANO
VINEYARDS AND WINERY, HEALDSBURG, DRY CREEK VALLEY.
THE WINERY GARDENS INCLUDE GEOMETRICALLY PLANNED
WALKWAYS AND FORMAL PARTERRES, AS WELL AS SOFTLY
CURVING PATHS AND COLORFUL HILLSIDES OF FLOWERS.

ABOVE AND RIGHT: NIEBAUM-COPPOLA ESTATE WINERY, RUTHERFORD, NAPA VALLEY.
AN ALLÉE OF TREES FRAMES A VIEW OF THE VINEYARD WHILE A LARGE, HEAVY ARBOR APPROPRIATELY
SETS OFF THE MASSIVE ARCHITECTURE OF THE WINERY.

RIGHT: AT THE KENDALL-JACKSON WINE
CENTER, SANTA ROSA, RUSSIAN RIVER VALLEY,
ORGANIC DEMONSTRATION GARDENS COMBINE
FORMAL EUROPEAN PARTERRES WITH INFORMAL
CALIFORNIA BEDDING PLANTS. ALONG THE SIDE
OF THE WINE CENTER, FOUR CULTURAL GARDENS
CONTAIN HERBS AND VEGETABLES FROM THE
CUISINES OF SOUTH AMERICA, FRANCE, ASIA, AND
ITALY. WINE SENSORY GARDENS SET OUT
HERB, FRUIT, AND VEGETABLE AFFINITIES FOR RED
AND WHITE WINES.

LEFT: THE GARDENS AT BENZIGER FAMILY WINERY, GLEN ELLEN, SONOMA VALLEY,
USE DROUGHT-RESISTANT PLANTS TO CREATE LANDSCAPES THAT CAN SURVIVE THE SIX MONTHS
WITHOUT RAIN WHILE PROVIDING COLORFUL BLOOM AND INTERESTING FOLIAGE.
ABOVE: THE ELEGANT WINDOW SHAPES AND VINE-COVERED BUILDINGS AND WALLS EVOKE
EUROPEAN GARDEN THEMES AT FRITZ WINERY, DRY CREEK VALLEY, CLOVERDALE,
BUT THE RAILROAD TIE ENTRYWAY UP PAST TERRACES OVERFLOWING WITH PLANTS IN
FULL FLOWER IS PURE CALIFORNIA DESIGN.

ABOVE: IN THE WINERY KITCHEN GARDEN AT ROBERT MONDAVI WINERY,
OAKVILLE, NAPA VALLEY, GRAVEL WALKWAYS AND RAISED BEDS EVOKE THE SENSE
OF CLASSIC PARTERRES COMBINING POPPIES, GARDEN VEGETABLES, AND FLOWERING
CABBAGES MUCH LIKE THE FAMOUS CHATEAU GARDEN OF VILLANDRY IN FRANCE.
RIGHT: THE GARDENS FLANKING THE ENTRANCE OF THE MISSION–STYLE
ST. FRANCIS WINERY & VINEYARDS, SANTA ROSA, SONOMA VALLEY, ARE SURROUNDED BY
HIGH STONE WALLS REMINISCENT OF SPANISH COURTYARDS.

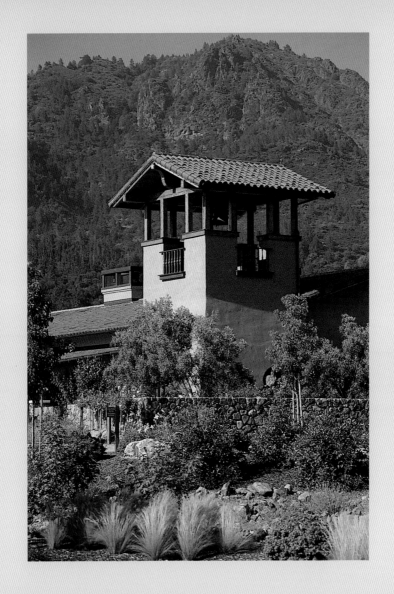

ABOVE AND RIGHT: FETZER VINEYARDS,
HOPLAND, MENDOCINO VALLEY, GROWS LONG
ROWS OF ORGANIC VEGETABLES FOR ITS
DEMONSTRATION KITCHEN AND COOKING CLASSES,
BUT ALWAYS IN CONJUNCTION WITH A RIOT OF
FLOWERS FOR A VISUAL FEAST.

LEFT AND ABOVE: COPIA, THE AMERICAN CENTER
FOR WINE, FOOD, & THE ARTS, NAPA, NAPA VALLEY. AS
AN EDUCATIONAL CENTER, THE GARDENS COMPLEMENT
THE LECTURES AND FOOD INFORMATION OFFERED INSIDE THE
BUILDING. SET OUT IN THE CLASSICAL MANNER OF A
GEOMETRIC GRID, STONEWORK DEFINES THE GARDEN BEDS,
ALTHOUGH LAWNS IN SOME BEDS INVITE THE SPECTATOR
IN FROM THE PATHS TO LOOK CLOSER AT THE PLANTS. MANY
UNUSUAL VEGETABLE, FRUIT, AND HERB PLANTS
ARE GROWN AND IDENTIFIED. MAPS OF THE GARDEN ARE
AVAILABLE FOR FURTHER INFORMATION.

ABOVE: TREFETHEN VINEYARDS, NAPA, NAPA VALLEY. THE LARGE BRICK COURTYARD
EVOKES A CARRIAGE DRIVEWAY. THE CLIPPED EVERGREENS IN LARGE TERRA-COTTA POTS CONTRAST
WITH THE SOFT, FINELY CUT LEAVES OF THE OLIVE TREES.

ABOVE: THE LUTHER BURBANK HOME AND GARDENS, SANTA ROSA, SONOMA COUNTY,
IS AN OASIS OF GREEN WITHIN THE BUSY CITY LIMITS. THE GARDENS ARE MAINTAINED WITH THE HELP OF
VOLUNTEERS, AND TOURS OF THE HOUSE AND GARDENS ARE AVAILABLE DAILY. THE GARDENS BURST WITH
PLANTS HYBRIDIZED BY LUTHER BURBANK, FROM SHASTA DAISIES TO THORNLESS CACTUS.

Water & Sculpture

PREVIOUS PAGES: GARDEN FOUNTAIN AT WILLIAM HILL WINERY, NAPA, NAPA VALLEY.

ABOVE: CHATEAU MONTELENA, CALISTOGA, NAPA VALLEY. REMINISCENT OF MONET'S

GIVERNY, A BRIDGE OVER A LAKE OFFERS THE SAME QUIET BEAUTY OF WATER, REFLECTION, AND FORM.

*P*onds and pools in the garden reflect the sky and clouds like rippling sculpture, and on a hot Wine Country day, cool the summer breeze for travelers. Classical Italian gardens always included the sound and spray of fountains or waterfalls, or water gurgled in troughs through the garden. Bamboo water flutes in Japanese gardens lilt with the music of gentle drips as accompaniment to the rustle of leaves.

Garden rooms seem more complete with furniture, whether garden urns, benches, or statuary. Sculpture along a garden path invites contemplation and lively discussion. Since the garden designer has taken pains to place a bench or sculpture in a niche to complement the view, garden visitors need only take time to pause and enjoy the sensory display.

LEFT AND ABOVE: CHATEAU ST. JEAN WINERY,
KENWOOD, SONOMA VALLEY. FOUNTAINS PROVIDE
AN OLD-WORLD FLAVOR TO THE LUSH SETTING
OF SPACIOUS LAWNS AND FLOWERING GARDENS.

ABOVE: MONOLITHIC FORMS CREATE A STARTLING
FOUNTAIN AT MATANZAS CREEK WINERY AND
ESTATE GARDENS, SANTA ROSA, SONOMA VALLEY.
RIGHT: A PLEASANT BENCH ALLOWS VISITORS TO
ENJOY THE CREEKSIDE GARDEN AND SCULPTURE
AT FERRARI-CARANO VINEYARDS AND WINERY,
HEALDSBURG, DRY CREEK VALLEY.

LEFT AND ABOVE: THE HAPPY TOAD WITH GOBLET IN HAND CAVORTS

ATOP WATER LILIES AT SCHRAMSBERG VINYARDS, CALISTOGA, NAPA VALLEY.

KNOWN AS THE *RIDDLER'S NIGHT OUT*, THE SCULPTURE PRESIDES OVER

THE FROG POND OUTSIDE THE TASTING ROOM OF THIS SPARKLING WINE CELLAR.

THE RESTORED AND REPLANTED GARDENS AT THE VICTORIAN

SCHRAM HOUSE REPLICATE THE ORIGINAL DESIGN, DATING FROM 1889.

ABOVE AND RIGHT: CHATEAU MONTELENA, CALISTOGA, NAPA VALLEY.

THE RED CHINESE BRIDGES TRAVERSING THE GARDENS LEAD OUT TO THE ISLANDS AND FOLLY ON JADE LAKE.

ABOVE: LEDSON WINERY AND VINEYARDS, KENWOOD, SONOMA VALLEY.
THE FOUNTAIN AT LEDSON WINERY IS SURROUNDED BY STANDARD WHITE ROSE TREES THAT
FRAME THE VIEW OF THE VINEYARDS.

ABOVE: LANDMARK VINEYARDS, KENWOOD, SONOMA VALLEY. COLUMNS OF DARK CYPRESS
EDGING A FOUNTAIN MIRROR THE STRUCTURE'S WATERY CYLINDRICAL SHAPE AND FRAME THE VIEW
OF THE VINEYARDS AND HILLSIDE BEYOND.

LEFT: TRANQUIL GARDEN POND AT DOMAINE CHANDON,
YOUNTVILLE, NAPA VALLEY.
ABOVE: CLINE CELLARS, SONOMA, CARNEROS.
JETS OF WATER, FOUNTAINS IN EFFECT WITH THE FUNCTION
OF AERATING THE PONDS, CREATE SHIMMERING WATER
SCULPTURES CONTRASTING WITH THE SMOOTH, STILL SURFACE.

ABOVE: COPPER SWANS LAND ON THE POND AT SEBASTIANI VINEYARDS
AND WINERY, SONOMA, SONOMA VALLEY. LOCATED IN THE TOWN OF SONOMA, THE WINERY'S IVY-STREWN
WALLS AND TALL CYPRESS RECALL ITS FOUNDER'S ITALIAN HERITAGE.
RIGHT AND FOLLOWING PAGES: FOUNTAINS AT FERRARI-CARANO VINEYARDS AND WINERY, HEALDSBURG, DRY
CREEK VALLEY, ARE SET IN CLASSICAL SETTINGS MINDFUL OF GARDENS IN ITALY, WITH FORMAL, GEOMETRIC
AXES. THE FOUNTAINS PROVIDE THE SOOTHING, COOLING ACCENT OF WATER SOUNDS.

LEFT: THE QUIET REFLECTION POOL AT MARKHAM VINEYARDS,
ST. HELENA, NAPA VALLEY, PROVIDES A MEDITATIVE ENVIRONMENT.
ABOVE: SET AMONG DAISIES AND PANSIES IN A QUIET SIDE GARDEN,
THE NAMESAKE OF THE WINERY WELCOMES HIS ANIMAL AND BIRD FRIENDS
TO ST. FRANCIS WINERY & VINEYARDS, SANTA ROSA, SONOMA VALLEY.

LEFT AND ABOVE: MODERN SCULPTURE
AND ITALIAN CYPRESS SURROUND THE CENTRAL
FOUNTAIN AT THE WINERY BUILT ON
THE BROW OF A HILL AT ARTESA VINEYARDS AND
WINERY, NAPA, CARNEROS.

LEFT: A FOUNTAIN PLANTED WITH REEDS LINES THE CENTRAL WALKWAY
TO CHIMNEY ROCK WINERY, NAPA, NAPA VALLEY.
ABOVE: A SPANISH–TILED FOUNTAIN FLANKS A WALKWAY AT ST. FRANCIS
WINERY & VINEYARDS, SANTA ROSA, SONOMA VALLEY.

ABOVE: A FOUNTAIN PROVIDES A FOCAL POINT
TO THE ENTRY COURTYARD OF FRANCISCAN OAKVILLE
ESTATE, RUTHERFORD, NAPA VALLEY.
RIGHT: THE POND AT THE ENTRANCE TO THE HESS
COLLECTION WINERY, NAPA, NAPA VALLEY,
CONTAINS A LARGE NUMBER OF WATER LILIES THAT
BLOOM FROM SPRING TO FALL.

ABOVE AND RIGHT: WITH ITS ITALIAN-STYLE COURTYARD, FOUNTAIN, AND STATUARY,

VIANSA WINERY & ITALIAN MARKETPLACE, SONOMA, CARNEROS,

LOOKS LIKE A TUSCAN HILLTOP TOWN BROUGHT TILE BY TILE TO CALIFORNIA.

IT IS ALSO HOME TO SONOMA COUNTY'S LARGEST MAN-MADE WETLANDS

AND NATURE PRESERVE AND FEATURES A VEGETABLE GARDEN ON THE GROUNDS, WHICH

SUPPLIES THE PRODUCTS SOLD IN THE MARKETPLACE.

PREVIOUS PAGES: THE ARCHITECTURE OF CLOS PEGASE,
CALISTOGA, NAPA VALLEY, IS COMPLEMENTED BY OUTDOOR SCULPTURE AND FORMAL GARDENS.
ABOVE AND RIGHT: THE SCULPTURE GARDEN AT AUBERGE DU SOLEIL,
NAPA, NAPA VALLEY, WINDS DOWN A SLOPING HILL, WITH TERRACES AND SHADY PATHS.
AFTER A STROLL THROUGH THE GARDENS, VISITORS CAN REST IN THE CAFÉ
OVERLOOKING THE BREATHTAKING NAPA VALLEY.

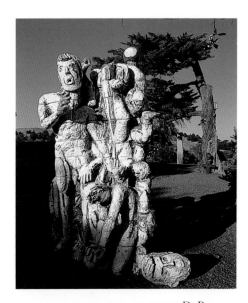

PREVIOUS PAGES, LEFT, AND ABOVE: DI ROSA
PRESERVE, NAPA, CARNEROS. MAKE AN
APPOINTMENT IN ADVANCE TO TOUR THE
GROUNDS, LUSHLY PLANTED WITH CALIFORNIA
NATIVES, AND VIEW THE ART COLLECTION, WITH
MANY EXAMPLES OF MODERN ART INSIDE AND OUT.

Flowers

PREVIOUS PAGES: ICELAND POPPIES AT FETZER VINEYARDS, HOPLAND, MENDOCINO VALLEY.

ABOVE: PURPLE WISTERIA CASCADES OVER AN ARBOR AT FERRARI-CARANO

VINEYARDS AND WINERY, HEALDSBURG, DRY CREEK VALLEY.

*W*ho does not love flowers? As a token of the renewal of the earth after a long winter, as a gift to the senses with their exuberant color, the silky texture of their leaves, and the fragrance of their bloom, flowers are joy incarnate.

The temperate climate of the Wine Country nurtures plants from all over the world, so that next to roses, a traveler might see South American daisies, or European sedums. Winter-blooming annuals come early in the spring. Iceland poppies with their crepelike petals herald spring bulbs and glorious flowering trees. As the seasons change, the flower parade marches on to irises, roses, summer annuals, and flowering shrubs. The seed plumes of grasses and fall-tinted leaves, as colorful as flowers, complete the year in the garden.

LEFT AND ABOVE: ORNAMENTAL PLUM TREES LINE
THE EDGE OF THE VINEYARD AND ENTRANCE
AT CLINE CELLARS, SONOMA, CARNEROS. LOOK FOR THE
SIX SPRING–FED PONDS AND THE BRIGHT GOLDEN
CARP THAT INHABIT THEM WHILE STROLLING THROUGH THE
GARDEN PLANTINGS OF ONE THOUSAND ROSE BUSHES.

LEFT: DAFFODILS AND BLOOMING FRUIT TREES ANNOUNCE SPRING AT THE
CHARLES KRUG WINERY, ST. HELENA, NAPA VALLEY.
ABOVE: FLOWERING PLUM TREES LINE THE EDGE OF THE WINERY AND VINEYARDS
IN SPRING AT CAKEBREAD CELLARS, RUTHERFORD, NAPA VALLEY.

ABOVE AND RIGHT: BERINGER VINEYARDS,
ST. HELENA, NAPA VALLEY. A MATURE SPRING-
FLOWERING DECIDUOUS MAGNOLIA TREE,
M. SOULANGIANA, IN FULL BLOOM. THE FALLEN
PETALS ON THE GROUND APPEAR AS ORNAMENTAL
AS THE FLOWERS ON THE TREE.

LEFT AND ABOVE: SPRING FLOWERS AT FERRARI-CARANO
VINEYARDS AND WINERY, HEALDSBURG, DRY CREEK VALLEY,
THICKLY PLANTED MUCH IN A STYLE SIMILAR TO THE
FRENCH CARPET PLANTING, SO NAMED BECAUSE THE PATTERN
OF COLORS WERE DESIGNED TO MIMIC PERSIAN
CARPETS. BLOOMING ORNAMENTAL TREES EDGE THE LAWN
IN FRONT OF THE WINERY.

ABOVE: FERRARI-CARANO VINEYARDS AND WINERY, HEALDSBURG, DRY CREEK VALLEY.

TULIPS MARCH ALONG THE EDGE OF A PATHWAY.

RIGHT: A BED OF ICELAND POPPIES AND DAFFODILS BLOOMING AT SUTTER HOME WINERY.

THE MILD WINTER WEATHER IN THE WINE COUNTRY ENCOURAGES BLOOMS

ALL WINTER LONG AND EARLY BULBS IN MARCH.

LEFT: PANSIES EDGE THE FLOWER BEDS AT SUTTER HOME WINERY, ST. HELENA, NAPA VALLEY.
BEHIND THEM, ICELAND POPPIES ALONG WITH THE LEAFY SPEARS OF BEARDED IRIS, PROMISE
LATER BLOOMS. THE SENTINEL PALM TREES ARE A CLASSIC FEATURE OF OLDER CALIFORNIA GARDENS.
ABOVE: BEARDED IRIS AT SPRING MOUNTAIN VINEYARD, ST. HELENA, NAPA VALLEY.

LEFT: THE POND AND CUPOLA AT FAR NIENTE
WINERY, OAKVILLE, NAPA VALLEY.
ABOVE: TULIPS BLOOM UNDERNEATH STANDARD ROSE
TREES AT NICKEL & NICKEL, OAKVILLE, NAPA VALLEY.
THE RESTORED 1880S FARMSTEAD OF JOHN C.
SULLENGER, GOLD, SILVER, AND QUICKSILVER MINE OWNER.
TOURS ARE BY APPOINTMENT ONLY AT THIS
SINGLE-VINEYARD WINERY.

ABOVE AND RIGHT: FAR NIENTE WINERY, OAKVILLE, NAPA VALLEY. THE EXTENSIVE,
THIRTEEN-ACRE GARDENS INCLUDE THE LARGEST PLANTING OF SOUTHERN AZALEAS IN CALIFORNIA
AND ARE OPEN BY APPOINTMENT ONLY FOR TOURS.

LEFT AND ABOVE: FAR NIENTE WINERY, OAKVILLE, NAPA VALLEY. IN SPRING, A SPECTACULAR SHOW OF AZALEAS, RHODODENDRONS, AND FLOWERING TREES FRAME THE WINERY, ORIGINALLY OPENED IN 1885. AFTER THEIR THREE YEAR RESTORATION, THE BUILDINGS WERE PLACED ON THE NATIONAL REGISTER OF HISTORIC PLACES.

ABOVE AND RIGHT: ROSES AND LAVENDER IN FULL BLOOM AT BRUTOCAO CELLARS,
HOPLAND, MENDOCINO VALLEY.

LEFT AND ABOVE: SPRING MOUNTAIN VINEYARD, ST. HELENA,
NAPA VALLEY. HOLLYHOCKS AND ROSES FRAME THE 1881 VICTORIAN VILLA
MIRAVALLE. GARDEN PATHS WIND AMONG PERENNIAL BEDS FEATURING
CLIMBING ROSES AND DROUGHT-TOLERANT RED-HOT POKER PLANTS.

ABOVE: SPRING MOUNTAIN VINEYARD, ST. HELENA,
NAPA VALLEY. A PATH WINDS THROUGH THE
LUSH, NEWLY RESTORED WINERY GARDENS. HIGH ON
THE MOUNTAIN, THE VALLEY VIEWS ARE SPECTACULAR.
RIGHT AND FOLLOWING PAGES: FETZER VINEYARDS, HOPLAND,
MENDOCINO VALLEY. THESE ORGANICALLY GROWN
GARDENS ARE DESIGNED TO ATTRACT A HOST OF BENEFICIAL
INSECTS, COMBINING HERBS, NATIVE PLANTS,
AND PERENNIALS IN A STUNNING DISPLAY OF COLOR,
FOLIAGE, AND FRAGRANCE.

LEFT AND ABOVE: CALIFORNIA POPPIES, THE STATE FLOWER, SPILL DOWN
A SLOPE AT THE RAYMOND BURR VINEYARDS, HEALDSBURG, DRY CREEK VALLEY.
WINERY FOUNDER, TELEVISION AND FILM STAR RAYMOND BURR WAS PASSIONATE
ABOUT ORCHIDS, AND SOME OF HIS COLLECTION IS STILL MAINTAINED AT THE WINERY.
TOURS OF THE ORCHID GREENHOUSE ARE OFTEN AVAILABLE.

RIGHT: VALLEY OF THE MOON WINERY, GLEN ELLEN, SONOMA VALLEY, SITS ON PROPERTY THAT WAS PART OF THE ORIGINAL LAND GRANT TO GENERAL VALLEJO. THE OWNERS HAVE RESTORED THE OLD STONE BUILDINGS ERECTED BY CHINESE LABORERS LOOKING FOR WORK AFTER THE COMPLETION OF THE TRANSCONTINENTAL RAILROAD. A THREE–HUNDRED–YEAR–OLD BAY TREE SHADES THE BUILDING. LOOK FOR THE PICNIC GROUNDS UNDERNEATH THE MAPLE AND PINE GROVES.

LEFT: MUMM NAPA VALLEY, RUTHERFORD, NAPA VALLEY. THE GARDENS AT MUMM
FEATURE DROUGHT–RESISTANT PERENNIALS NEXT TO THE ENTRY WALKWAY.
ABOVE: SILVERADO VINEYARDS, NAPA VALLEY. IN SPRING, THE TERRACED FLOWER BEDS
BURST WITH DAISIES, ICELAND POPPIES, AND PANSIES.

ABOVE AND RIGHT: KORBEL CHAMPAGNE CELLARS,
GUERNEVILLE, RUSSIAN RIVER VALLEY.
KORBEL BEGAN PRODUCING SPARKLING WINES IN
1882, AND THE EXTENSIVE GARDENS AROUND
THE CELLARS ARE FILLED WITH PLANTS
BELOVED OF THE OWNERS. THERE ARE SPECIAL
COMPLIMENTARY GARDEN TOURS AS WELL
AS TOURS OF THE CELLARS.

LEFT, ABOVE, AND FOLLOWING PAGES:
FERRARI–CARANO VINEYARDS AND WINERY,
HEALDSBURG, DRY CREEK VALLEY. PROPRIETOR
RHONDA CARANO LOVES HEIRLOOM
AND DAVID AUSTIN ROSES, AND SHE PLANTED
THE SPECTACULAR ROSES AT THE WINERY
NAMED "VILLA FIORE" TO BLOOM IN THE
GARDENS FROM SPRING UNTIL FALL.

Artesa Vineyards and Winery
1345 Henry Rd.
Napa, CA 94559
707-224-1668
www.artesawinery.com

Auberge du Soleil
180 Rutherford Hill Rd.
Rutherford, CA 94573
800-348-5406
www.aubergedusoleil.com

Benziger Family Winery
1883 London Ranch Rd.
Glen Ellen, CA 95442
888-490-2739
www.benziger.com

Beringer Vineyards
2000 Main St.
St. Helena, CA 94574
707-963-7115
www.beringer.com

Brutocao Cellars
13500 Hwy. 101
Hopland, CA 95449
800-433-3689
www.brutocaocellars.com

Cakebread Cellars
8300 Hwy. 29
Rutherford, CA 94573
800-588-0298
707-963-5222
www.cakebread.com

Charles Krug Winery
2800 Main St.
St. Helena, CA 94574
800-682-KRUG (5784)
www.charleskrug.com

Chateau Montelena
1429 Tubbs Ln.
Calistoga, CA 94515
707-942-5105
www.montelena.com

Chateau St. Jean Winery
8555 Hwy. 12
Kenwood, CA 95452
707-833-4134
www.chateaustjean.com

Chateau Souverain Winery
400 Souverain Rd.
Geyserville, CA 95441
888-80-WINES (9-4637)
www.chateausouverain.com

Chimney Rock Winery
5350 Silverado Trail
Napa, CA 94558
707-257-2641
www.chimneyrock.com

Cline Cellars
24737 Hwy. 121
Sonoma, CA 95476
800-546-2070
707-940-4000
www.clinecellars.com

Clos Pegase
1060 Dunaweal Ln.
Calistoga, CA 94515
707-942-4981
www.clospegase.com

Copia, The American Center
for Wine, Food & the Arts
500 First St.
Napa, CA 94559
800-51-COPIA (2-6742)
707-259-1600
www.copia.org

di Rosa Preserve
5200 Carneros Hwy. 121
Napa, CA 94559
707-226-5991
www.dirosapreserve.org

Domaine Carneros
1240 Duhig Rd.
Napa, CA 94559
707-257-0101
www.domainecarneros.com

Domaine Chandon
1 California Dr.
Yountville, CA 94599
707-944-2280
www.chandon.com

Far Niente Winery
1350 Acacia Dr.
Oakville, CA 94562
707-944-2861
www.farniente.com

Ferrari-Carano Vineyards
and Winery
8761 Dry Creek Rd.
Healdsburg, CA 95448
800-831-0381
707-433-6700
www.ferrari-carano.com

Fetzer Vineyards
13601 East Side Rd.
Hopland, CA 95440
800-846-8637
707-744-1250
www.fetzer.com

Franciscan Oakville Estate
1178 Galleron Rd.
Rutherford, CA 94573
707-963-7111
www.franciscan.com

Fritz Winery
24691 Dutcher Creek Rd.
Cloverdale, CA 95425
800-418-9463
707-894-3389
www.fritzwinery.com

The Hess Collection Winery
4411 Redwood Rd.
Napa, CA 94558
707-255-1144, ext. 237
www.hesscollection.com

Kendall-Jackson Wine Center
5007 Fulton Rd.
Fulton, CA 95439
707-571-7500
www.kj.com

Korbel Champagne Cellars
13250 River Rd.
Guerneville, CA 95446
707-824-7000
www.korbel.com

Landmark Vineyards
101 Adobe Canyon Rd.
Kenwood, CA 95452
707-833-0053
www.landmarkwine.com

Ledson Winery and Vineyards
7335 Hwy. 12
Kenwood, CA 95409
707-537-3810
www.ledson.com

Luther Burbank Home
and Gardens
Corner of Santa Rosa Ave. and
Sonoma Ave.
Santa Rosa, CA 95404
707-524-5445
www.lutherburbank.org

Markham Vineyards
2812 St. Helena Hwy. North
St. Helena, CA 94574
707-963-5292
www.markhamvineyards.com

Matanzas Creek Winery and
Estate Gardens
6097 Bennett Valley Rd.
Santa Rosa, CA 95404
800-590-6464
www.matanzascreek.com

MUMM NAPA VALLEY
8445 Silverado Trail
Rutherford, CA 94573
707-967-7700
www.mummnapavalley.com

NEWTON VINEYARD
2555 Madrona Ave.
St. Helena, CA 94574
707-963-9000
www.newtonvineyard.com

NICKEL & NICKEL
8164 Hwy. 29
Oakville, CA 94562
707-967-9600
www.nickelandnickel.com

NIEBAUM-COPPOLA ESTATE WINERY
1991 St. Helena Hwy.
Rutherford, CA 94573
800-RUBICON (782-4266)
707-968-1100
www.niebaum-coppola.com

OSMOSIS–THE ENZYME BATH SPA
209 Bohemian Hwy.
Freestone, CA 95472
707-823-8231
www.osmosis.com

RAYMOND BURR VINEYARDS
8339 West Dry Creek Rd.
Healdsburg, CA 95448
707-433-8559
www.raymondburrvineyards.com

ROBERT MONDAVI WINERY
7801 St. Helena Hwy.
Oakville, CA 94562
888-RMONDAVI (766-6328),
ext. 2000
707-968-2000
www.robertmondaviwinery.com

ST. FRANCIS WINERY
& VINEYARDS
100 Pythian Rd.
Santa Rosa, CA 95409
800-543-7713
707-833-4666
www.stfranciswine.com

SCHRAMSBERG VINEYARDS
1400 Schramsberg Rd.
Calistoga, CA 94515
707-942-4558
www.schramsberg.com

SEBASTIANI VINEYARDS
AND WINERY
389 Fourth St. East
Sonoma, CA 95476
707-933-3200
www.sebastiani.com

SILVERADO VINEYARDS
6121 Silverado Trail
Napa, CA 94575
707-257-1770
www.silveradovineyards.com

SPRING MOUNTAIN VINEYARD
2805 Spring Mountain Rd.
St. Helena, CA 94574
707-967-4188
www.springmountainvineyard.com

SUTTER HOME WINERY
277 St. Helena Hwy.
St. Helena, CA 94574
707-963-3104
www.sutterhome.com

TREFETHEN VINEYARDS
1160 Oak Knoll Ave.
Napa, CA 94558
707-255-7700
www.trefethen.com

V. SATTUI WINERY
1111 White Ln.
St. Helena, CA 94574
707-963-7774
www.vsattui.com

VALLEY OF THE MOON WINERY
777 Madrone Rd.
Glen Ellen, CA 95442
707-996-6941
www.valleyofthemoon.com

VIANSA WINERY & ITALIAN
MARKETPLACE
25200 Arnold Dr.
Sonoma, CA 95476
800-995-4740
707-935-4700
www.viansa.com

WILLIAM HILL WINERY
1761 Atlas Peak Rd.
Napa, CA 94558
707-224-4477
www.williamhill.com

FOLLOWING PAGE: ICELAND POPPIES AT
SUTTER HOME WINERY, ST. HELENA, NAPA VALLEY.

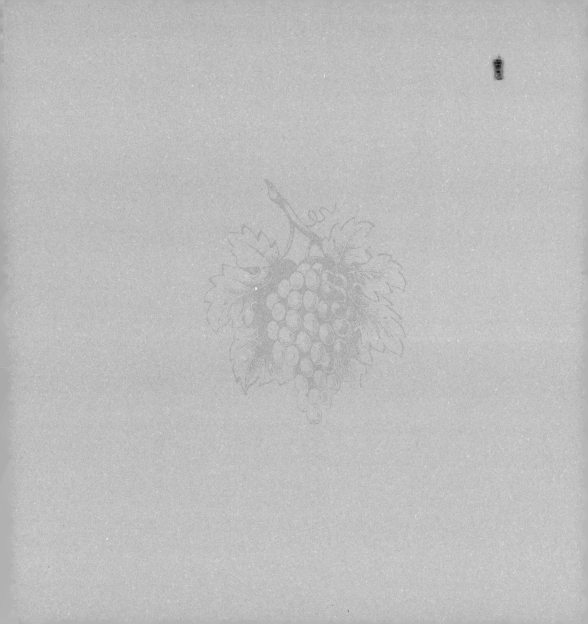